On the Shoulders of Men

Introduction

One of the most misunderstood people I have ever met made the most sense to me, once while in class the classroom bully told me it isn't that you are disliked it's that people fear what they disassociate with what they don't understand.

Powerful enough of a statement to have lasted my entire adult life and yet so elementary and accurate. As with many of us we spend years of our lives trying to find our identities, whether it is modeling ourselves after sports figures, actors, scholars, or in my case Theologians in order to help us to define and refine the person that we would like to be.

~2 Corinthians 13:11 "Finally, brothers and sisters, rejoice! Strive for full restoration, encourage one another, be of one mind, live in peace. And the God of love and peace will be with you."

Psalm 127:3–5

Behold, children are a heritage from the LORD, the fruit of the womb a reward.
Like arrows in the hand of a warrior are the children of one's youth.
Blessed is the man who fills his quiver with them!
He shall not be put to shame when he speaks with his enemies in the gate.

Chapter One

It isn't until we have gone through some of these ups and downs in life that the person, we were trying to transform into comes to be the person we actually are, and the vision seldom aligns with the reality.

So, it is for many young men in the world today, struggling to adapt to a world that refuses to slow down and wait for us to mature and comprehend the place where we are and the things that we are having to grasp.

The pressures are always building and sometimes we just look for a way to release the stress and the anxiety, the pressures of this world only build they never fully go away.

Even the most adapted young man is constantly adjusting and improving upon themselves to stay ahead. And so, the young mind is ever developing and always questioning the place where they are in society which brings me to the meaning of his book. On the Shoulders of Men is an observance from the vantage point of a young African American male raised by a single mother who through all of the pressure and growing pains managed to figure out enough of his life to become a man during the time when life expectancy did not exceed the age of sixteen.

And systems of bondage and confusion were created to slow down progress and development of young men from impoverished communities.

~ For when you make a mistake and need to apologize.
Ephesians 6:4 "Fathers, do not exasperate your children; instead, bring them up in the training and instruction of the Lord."

Chapter Two

According to a 2018 census 24 million children younger than 18 are living with an unmarried parent. Most (15 million) are living with a solo mother.

~Acts 2:17

In the last days, God says, I will pour out my Spirit on all people. Your sons and daughters will prophesy, your young men will see visions, your old men will dream dreams.

This topic has been a long time coming, I would like to say that it is my life's work being that I am a living subject that has personally had this experience. There are many different views on single parenting taught and written about from various views by many very authoritative voices in today's psychology and Counseling communities. However, I have yet to see one of them address single parenthood from the view that I would like to discuss. The viewpoint I'm expressly speaking of the view of the child, specifically the male child being born into the home with a mother. This has become more and more the norm as the structure of families has become more fluid, men and women have less interest in staying together or even becoming husband and wife. The family structure has been broken and although many have managed to maintain their tradition beliefs many have justified the need to be apart and raise children on their own.

~ For when you need to forgive.
Colossians 3:13 “Bear with each other and forgive one another if any of you has a grievance against someone. Forgive as the Lord forgave you.”

Statistics by race ethnicity and family nativity Data from 2019 indicates:
-Black and American Indian kids are most likely to live in a single parent family (64%of black children and 52% of American Indian children fit this demographic.
-White, an Asian and Pacific Islander kids are least likely to live in a single parent household.
-Latino children and children who identify as two or more races fall somewhere in the middle with 40% of these kids living in single parent households.

~ For when you need strength.
Isaiah 41:10 “So do not fear, for I am with you; do not be dismayed, for I am your God. I will strengthen you and help you; I will uphold you with my righteous right hand.

Chapter Three

Men who are raised by single mothers know how be taken care of but they rarely know how to treat or take care of women. Men learn by example and that example comes from watching how men treat women not how women treat men.

~ For when you need to say no.

1 Corinthians 15:58 “Be steadfast, immovable, always abounding in the work of the Lord.

Parenting is hard enough for a mother and a father and raising children has never been an easy task, from Pampers to Graduation the ins and outs of raising children is complicated. Many young men in this scenario can scarcely recall a time when there was a father around because mainly these men decided that they did not want to be in a relationship that required that level of commitment. These things are never explained to children in fact negative stories that cause bad memories like this are kept from many children until they are old enough to actually understand the entire situation. Sometimes they never get an understanding of the situation.

~ For when you need wisdom.

Proverbs 4:6-7, “Do not forsake wisdom, and she will protect you; love her, and she will watch over you. Wisdom is supreme; therefore, get wisdom. Though it cost all you have, get understanding.”

There is the obvious confusion that comes from watching your friends that actually have their fathers in their lives interact with one another. Gleaning what you can from their interactions with their fathers, holding onto every guiding word that comes from older respected men in your community becomes a way of life. Hearing your friends discuss how their dads would always be either at work, eating first or sleeping because they had to go to work in the morning.

These Fatherless sons stand on the sideline and watch as they play catch, work on cars on even small things like cutting the lawn. This is a dangerous time for these young men, young boys as they are attempting to understand and grow, they are forced or expected to automatically morph into a man with no direction and no template to pattern themselves after just a jumbled bunch of memories of others and the actions that they had with their father.

Chapter Four

~ For when you need joy in your home.
Psalm 63:6-7 "For you have been my help, and in the shadow of your wings I will sing for joy. My soul clings to you; your right hand upholds me."

So let me start there with this portion of time that I capture will group the younger years to preteen. This is a challenging time for young boys because there a lot of things going on emotionally as well as physically. There are obvious things that a single mother really does not think about. Things that a single mother may not know herself. Things like just desiring to wait until your son is older to discuss the male anatomy, that doesn't mean that their bodies will wait for you to feel comfortable enough to discuss this.

~ For when you doubt.
Proverbs 3:5-8 "Trust in the Lord with all your heart and lean not on your own understanding; in all your ways submit to him, and he will make your paths straight. Do not be wise in your own eyes; fear the Lord and shun evil. This will bring health to your body and nourishment to your bones."

In fact, it is negligent to not discuss this with your sons there should be a level of trust and comfort with your sons in this situation you have to really develop a relationship with your son. Flipping this, as the son you feel rejected that you are having all of these emotional and physical occurrences in your body that you don't understand. Potty training seems like where all of this stops for a lot of single parent households, but it is only the beginning there are many who learn to use the bathroom standing on their own with no assistance from their mothers.

For the most part ruining walls and the tiles around the toilet until they get a better understanding of what they are trying to do all the while thinking this is something they must do. I recall a time in my life during elementary school when I first realized how pretty little girls where. Truth is they were always pretty, but my focus had never been on them, and I had never seen them as girls just other kids that didn't have to stand in the free lunch line.

~For when you are afraid.
John 14:27 – "Peace I leave with you; my peace I give to you. Not as the world gives do I give to you. Let not your hearts be troubled, neither let them be afraid.

Chapter Five

My mother would say things to deter my interest but that's not a normal and healthy approach to human behavior but it's normal for single mothers not relating to their sons. This is deflecting, placing your feelings in the place of your sons' feelings will leave them holding back information in order to not offend you and appearing to be the good son.

Personally, I found myself awkward around girls and for a kid that did not verbally communicate well with others it was even worse when they spoke to me. I wasn't shy I was not experienced in talking to others. I had two sisters one older one younger and conversation with them seemed normal anything outside of that felt forced, I didn't know how to express myself, it became worse over time when the rest of my body became alert to my feelings, and this is still pre-puberty.

~ For when you need grace and need to extend it.
2 Corinthians 12:9 "And He has said to me, 'My grace is sufficient for you, for power is perfected in weakness.' Most gladly, therefore, I will rather boast about my weaknesses, so that the power of Christ may dwell in me."

Sometimes school can be a painful place for a young boy growing up without guidance without a father. There are things that you are excluded from just because you have no father and consequently you are not expected to be good in many things that seem to come natural to some of the other boys.

Being called up to speak in front of the class at the wrong time, when you are trying to figure out why you are having an erection and having to leave class quickly when the bell rings at the wrong time, being told to stand up and answer questions in class at the wrong time, all of these things can cause a young boy to think something is wrong with them.

Chapter Six

~ For when you are angry.
I Peter 4:8-11 "Above all, love each other deeply, because love covers over a multitude of sins. Offer hospitality to one another without grumbling."

Having to hide your private parts or else become embarrassed because you have never been told how to control yourself. No one has taken the time to explain to you that these are natural and normal things that happen. I know for a long time I thought I was broken, and there was no way to communicate this to my mother because she was going through her own struggle of adulthood, learning to raise children on her own, with only one of them being a boy and having to work several jobs to support the family alone made her less of a nurturing mother and more of a provider. Many young men from this demographic suffer with long term emotional effects.

~ For when you are heartbroken.
John 16:33 "These things I have spoken to you, that in Me you may have peace. In the world you will have tribulation; but be of good cheer, I have overcome the world."

In spite of a mother's effort to be present for their sons most of these boys feel incomplete and lack a sense of identity. This void is what causes many young men to act out of disrespect to the situation in which they are being reared in. Some results are violent acts, intentional disrespect and in many cases aligning with the wrong crowd in order to find a sense of belonging to something. Young men crave the attention of other men in order to validate themselves as equal men regardless of not having a father in their lives. These sons are predisposed toward physiological disturbances. While this may be destructive it is the way many of them cope with the absence of male guidance and a father figure.

~ For when you need peace.
Matthew 5:9 "Blessed are the peacemakers, for they will be called children of God."
Sometimes the role and everything that a single mother has to deal with shapes them and creates an identity to this new reality that they are faced with but the effect on the son is forever written on their heart. They are constantly searching for their place well into manhood.

Chapter Seven

~ For when you are frustrated.
Psalm 133:1 “How good and pleasant it is when God’s people live together in unity!”

Many parents don’t understand the power to change destinies with the words they speak. Many times things are said that shape a person or breaks a person. A young mind can be broken by insults or by things said from a place of pain. So naturally avoidance and unnecessary confrontation becomes the norm. because the son does not want to become the unvalued male, or worthless man that he constantly hears his single mother discussing. This is not the case in all households, but this is the case in many. These scars are deep they cut to the very core of the young male being raised in this environment. And in some cases, these words shape the identity of the person they will become either strengthening them or tearing down the identity or idea of what it means to be a man.

~ For when you are confused.
1 Corinthians 14:33 – “For God is not the author of confusion, but of peace, as in all churches of the saints.”

Time is not a good indication of how soon a young male heals from the trauma they experienced growing up in a single parent household. In most cases the laws protecting women’s rights to custody prevent Fathers from automatically becoming the parent that children reside with. There is no formal training for parents to attend where they learn how to properly raise a child, but many believe that a woman has natural maternal instincts.

~ For when you need community.
Hebrews 10:24-25 "And let us consider how we may spur one another on toward love and good deeds, not giving up meeting together, as some are in the habit of doing, but encouraging one another."

This I will agree to however that in no way means that all women are capable of Fathering a son, raising a man is not the same as Fathering a son.
There is the exception those that have had a Man in their lives, a role model a father, a mom's boyfriend good or bad the risk that comes along with this is that the habits the actions and the ways that male role model acted becomes embedded in the young son who is gleaning all that he can from the man.

Chapter Eight

Many of these young men become socially awkward it comes natural for obvious reasons like not knowing the rules to sports like football and baseball, there isn't a place to go to sign up for a dad substitute.in my own case I learned to ride my first bike because my older sister loved me enough to patiently push me around the apartment complex until I got it.

There was no proud father there to cheer me on, there was no mother there to embrace my accomplishment because she was working, just the proud smile of an older sister who I had bothered to the point where she wanted to help me.
Graduating at the top of my class and looking for the approval of a man a father was never an option so naturally I went to the one place I knew that I would learn to become a man the US Military.

For me this was an easy choice but for others they may have not felt this need for validation. For many childhoods psychologist the focus has never been on how the son raised in a single household family view the family, it has been what ere the effects on the son. Many sons see the family as a place where they are not valued where their opinions don't make sense and their place in the family questionable at best.

The absence of the Father in black households creates a vacuum that the young son, unlearned about manhood, untaught about being a boy now feels he must try to fulfill all while knowing he is an outsider living on the inside.

~ For when you are worried.

Matthew 11:28-30 "Come to me, all you who are weary and burdened, and I will give you rest. Take my yoke upon you and learn from me, for I am gentle and humble in heart, and you will find rest for your souls. For my yoke is easy and my burden is light."

Chapter Nine

Most states required that boys had a separate room from girls which causes even more strain on some households living in these poorer conditions. Children have separation anxiety also, when children bond with one another it is normal for them to become codependent on one another. All I had ever known is sharing a room with my older sister and although she needed space from me, I didn't know how to separate myself from her, I slept with the light on in the bedroom out of fear that I was alone. That the very person I knew would always be there was being taken away from me. Young boys left to their own thoughts can be trouble, I quickly became the sleep deprived little boy because I was afraid to be alone. The solution was my sister tape recorder wouldn't you know it almost instinctively she would bring her tape recorder to me at night, and I could play her cassette tapes low until I fell asleep.

~ For when you don't know what to do.

Ephesians 4:2-3
"Be completely humble and gentle; be patient, bearing with one another in love. Make every effort to keep the unity of the Spirit through the bond of peace."

Although the focus and perspective are on how single parenting affects young boys there is an obvious effect on young girls also. My sisters are proof of that very thing.
Many times, young boys going through this type of situation turn out to be delinquent or sometimes they struggle with their gender because they become what they are surrounded by. This is not understood or even discussed by many in the child psychological field because they see the person as damaged and a project to be fixed rather than human in pain, however they aren't able to understand what shaped these actions. In order to understand this, you have to understand the why. Universal laws require a reaction to every action if this being the case societal pressures created this need for all women to have children prepared or not. There should never be an expectation that women have to have children this should be optional however women without children are looked down on and called infertile or barren.

These sons these fatherless boys are not projects, these are young impressionable boys that have no guidance from a male figure. Although many go through their childhood learning bits and pieces of what many would consider lessons, what they have actually learned is to imitate behaviors.

Chapter Ten

Many watch the way their uncles walked with a proud little dip in their strides, some call it striding, stick your chest out pull your shoulders back stand tall these things are rehearsed until they become seamless. I practiced and practiced walking the way they did in my bedroom for what seemed like hours and never really mastered it, and never found out why they called it pimping either. The point is that because there was no male in the house, I naturally latched on to whatever I saw other men doing.

~ For when you need patience.
Romans 12:12 “Be joyful in hope, patient in affliction, faithful in prayer.”

Boys, especially, need a present father. He is going to set their concept of what a man is. Dad will be the first standard of masculinity in a child’s life, and he’ll be the one with the longest-lasting impact.

One of the most important things boys learn from their dads is how to treat a woman. When kids grow up, they tend to emulate their parents’ marriage. If mom and dad fought a lot, had affairs, and got divorced young, there’s a high chance their kids’ marriages will go the same way. When mom and dad treat each other with respect, kids learn how to do the same with their own partners.

In fact, boys are more likely to emulate their fathers if their parents have a good relationship. Part of the reason a child wants to be like his father is because he wants his mother’s love. If a boy can see that his parents are in love, he’ll imitate his father more. If dad isn’t present, boys will still come with up a concept of manliness. They just won’t get it from their parents. They’ll get from TV.

There are many myths surrounding the young fatherless son and the mother who does her best to raise him. Despite her trying there will be a void in the teaching because relating is not reaching.
Many mothers in this situation do what they feel is best for their families and although they do their best the love the show the other sibling daughters may never reach the level of love for the son.

Chapter Eleven

Many naturally assume that a young man who was raised by their mother will be a bad parent themselves because there was no one that taught them how to be a good man. That is assuming that all men are good men, truth is that the young man may have problems showing his emotions or teaching his son love because these are things that he himself may have never experienced. But not having a mother is not a Litmus test for a man's ability to Father.

~For when the future is daunting.
Matthew 6:34 "Therefore do not worry about tomorrow, for tomorrow will worry about its own things. Sufficient for the day is its own trouble."

There was a book mobile that would come into our neighborhood every month where kids could get on board and check out books and return others, they even had a space where you could sit and read until it was time for them to leave. This quickly became the safe place for me. I loved to read I was alone a lot as a child so the way I passed time was reading. I began reading books about sports figures like Jackie Robinson, Babe Ruth, Muhammad Ali, Sugar Ray Robinson, whatever I could get my hands on really, I wanted to be a football player because they seemed to be accepted by everyone.
Every child has a safe place and a place where they feel they can forget the pressures they face; part of the issue is sometimes parents don't see that children do carry stress and the pressures that they are under can sometimes be insurmountable to them.

Some communities have Parent assistance groups like the big brothers' organizations that exist in some cities, but the daily needs of these young men are rarely even discussed since many of these program mentors have their own families to focus on.

This may seem like it's not a big deal but when you are a young boy struggling with your identity you need that time to be around other boys to build you up and help your confidence. There is almost an expectation that these young boys will be alright, and the truth is these young men are growing up damaged and told they need to succeed.

Chapter Twelve

Many sons in this scenario struggle with understanding the reason behind being raised by a woman they are casualties of a relationship that went bad but never explained. Many Mothers never discuss or explain this to their sons but there are many that do. How is it our society has brushed this issue aside as if it is normal this is puzzling to me a child that grew up lacking the influence of his father how is it expected to follow the role of a male that he has never seen.

Radical change is needed to not only understand how to properly communicate but how to express love for these young men. Many single parent's fall in this area because they have never experienced parental love themselves but there are no excuses that can be made for not giving our children the love and nurturing that they deserve.

As a young boy I couldn't understand why I became bitter as I went to the football field in the evening to watch the other boys put on their equipment and train I would take a book with me and pretend to read if I saw the other boys looking at me in the bleachers. I didn't want them to think it bothered me that I couldn't play, and I would leave and get home before they were released from practice so they wouldn't question me on the way home.

What's interesting to me is that many men grow up in a two-parent household and they grow up with all of the privilege of having more than one parent influence in their lives and shape who they become. So that is twice the love even if one of the parents is usually not as loving as the other. That's two parents that you have access too when you are trying to make a decision and need guidance. That means you have a much better chance of not being raised in a broken household, and by broken, I mean that to say a untraditional family structure.

There are things that you may miss out on by being a son of a single mother that other young boys your age will never have to experience. Of all the things that I believe I missed is the feeling of safety and protection. Not knowing if you were safe at night and double checking the doors just so you will feel secure at night were issues for me. I would catch myself looking out windows throughout the house or staring out of the peep hole in the door that led to the hallway of our apartment building. While others would call this nosey, I would call this a fearful nervous reaction to a situation that I could not control. I was very much what most would call a nervous kid, and I am sure that this feeling of insecurity is common for young boys in this situation.

Chapter Thirteen

There is something comforting about knowing that a man is there in the household to protect you, even if this is not necessarily the case that a father is the protector, he is the masculine figure that provides a feeling of security. There is a certain relief of responsibility for a young boy knowing that the job of being a man can be done by a man and not something that he has to do. My mother had this kitchen knife that she got from Tupperware she really loved this knife it had a jagged side that could be used to tear open aluminum cans if needed and then a sharp side that resembled any other knife. I decided that if this could tear open a can it could definitely be used to protect our family. So, I got my hands on the knife and placed it in the springs under my bed so that I would have access to it if needed. It was just another weapon to add to my home-made arsenal, I had the nun chucks with the bent nails holding the chain down, an old kitchen mop stick which I decorated with sky blue electric tape and a shuriken (Chinese star) that I got from the comic bookstore up the street.

The point is not that I had an arsenal of items that I thought I would protect our family with, the point is that I felt it was my responsibility as a child to do so. I was made to feel that this was my job, all of the duties that are expected for males to do, taking out the trash, carrying grocery bags, lifting boxes, taking up for your sisters and protecting the household were things that were expected from me.

So many little boys are going through this today. It's not uncommon to see little boys dragging trash cans to the dumpsters in apartment complexes, what many don't see is that many times that little boy has to find someone to help him lift the trash can into the dumpster to dump it.
Many times, the young boy learns what he sees he picks up on cooking and cleaning doing laundry and other things that aren't traditionally considered things a male should do but it is what he sees so it becomes what he knows.

There are many things that shape us to become who we are and when we overlook the root of a problem the problem continues to grow. It is paramount to the growth of these young men that they are given the opportunity to live in a two-parent household if possible. As I stated earlier a woman can raise a man, she just can't show him how to be one. The key word being SHOW in this case.

Chapter Fourteen

We as parents have to learn to be open and learn to be understanding this comes by listening to our children, it is my perspective that this is especially true in single parent households where a son is being raised by a mother.

The Bible is full of examples that guide our understanding and the life that God requires from us. The challenges of parenting can be hard, the challenges of being a single parent can be overwhelming. There is no perfect fix but many perspectives on this what we as parents see as good parenting is not the same view as the view of our children. However, with patience, prayer and guidance from God.

A prayer for your son's discernment

Lord, I pray that my son will develop an eternal perspective and purpose, not an earthly one. Help him to see life–and every challenge–through Your eyes, eager and unafraid to share with others the good news of Jesus wherever he goes. I pray that they will set his minds on things above, not just what's going on here, and that he will be rooted and grounded in Your love. I pray that he will come to understand the extent of Your own love for him–that it surpasses all the head knowledge they will acquire in school. I pray he will be filled up with You from morning 'til night.

A prayer for your own wisdom

Lord, Your Word says "If any of you lacks wisdom, he should ask God, who gives generously to all without finding fault, and it will be given to him" (James 1:5). Lord, I need that kind of wisdom to know when to speak to my son and when to be silent. "Do not let any unwholesome talk, lecturing, judging, or accusing come of my mouth, but only what is helpful for building my son up according to their needs, that it may benefit those who listen" (Eph. 4:29). Let me also be "quick to listen, slow to speak and slow to become angry, for my anger doesn't bring about the righteous life that God desires" (James 1:19).

A prayer for a son who has turned from God

Dear God, You know our hearts, you hear our prayers, and care about all that concerns us. You understand the burden we carry and how we want, more than anything, to see our loved ones come to you. Help us to remember that you love them more than we ever could. And you desire to extend your great love and forgiveness, your mercy and hope. Thank you that nothing is too difficult for you. Thank you that your power is unlimited, and you came to set the captives free. Thank you that you wait, arms open, for the prodigal to return, that you look for his arrival to lavishly celebrate that he's come home. We praise you for you are Redeemer and Rescuer, Savior and Lord. We know and believe that there's no pit so deep that your love can't reach us still. We understand that your mercies are new every morning, and your faithfulness is great.

Lord, we ask that you halt the plans of the enemy over these we love as we bring them before you right now. We pray that his schemes be demolished and that your plans for good, for a future and hope, would prevail. Would you open blind eyes that they might see your Truth. Would you rescue those walking in darkness and heal the deep wounds of those who've been hurt.

We pray for the miraculous intervention of your Spirit to draw them to yourself, to work strong on behalf of our loved ones who are lost and wandering. For you came with good news, to heal the brokenhearted, to proclaim freedom for captives and release for the prisoners. Though we deserved penalty for our wrong, you stood in our place and took the blows on our behalf. You choose to die, so that we can live. Forever and free.

Lord, forgive our unbelief. Forgive the times we've doubted that you could ever change a distant heart. Forgive our hard-heartedness, our weariness, or forgetfulness to "pray continually." Thank you that you never give up on us. Remind us of how you've changed our own hearts. How your miracle of life and hope has sprung up deep within our souls. We love you Lord, we need you, and we thank you that you hear our prayers and are at work even now. Powerfully. Faithfully. Miraculously. Thank you for the gift of our Savior, God with us. Thank you for your goodness and love. In Jesus' Name, Amen.

Scriptural prayers for your son

1. Create in my son a clean heart, O God, and renew a right spirit within him (Psalm 51:10).
2. May my son walk after You, God, and fear You and keep Your commandments and obey Your voice. May he serve You and hold fast to You (Deuteronomy 13:4).
3. May my son be strong and courageous and not fear or be in dread, for it is You, Lord, our God, who goes with him. You will never leave him or forsake him (Deuteronomy 31:6).
4. May my son walk before You, God, as King David walked, with integrity of heart and uprightness, doing according to all that You have commanded him, and keeping Your statutes and rules (1 Kings 9:4).
5. Like Timothy, may my son be an example to believers in speech, in conduct, in love, in faith, and in purity (1 Timothy 4:12).

A prayer for your son's relationships and influences

First, oh Lord, forgive us for the times when we have misplaced our priorities so that we haven't been available to model a strong relationship with You in front of our kids. Help us to understand the power of our influence in our children's lives and to reorder our schedule so that we can be available to both directly and indirectly offer the godly influence that our sons desperately need.

Second, while we do pray that our sons would be protected from negative influences, we also pray that you would surround them with friendships and mentor-type relationships that portray what it means to have an authentic relationship with Christ. In turn, we pray that you would raise our sons up to be the influencers of the next generation. We pray that you would allow godliness and righteousness to dwell in their hearts so richly that these evidences of your truth spill out of them and to every person they encounter.

A prayer for your son's body image and purity

Dear Jesus, we weep with you over the number of our kids who are buying into the lie that sexual pleasure is something to experiment with. We pray that our sons would treasure their sexuality as a true gift from You, and that they would honor that gift by saving it as a precious treasure to give their future spouse. We ask that you help them to be strong in the face of their own desires and that they would choose purity in the face of temptation. Lord we also ask that you'd protect our sons from the idea that they must do anything and everything (including abusing their bodies through eating disorders, drug abuse, or other harmful behaviors) in order to attaining a “preferred” shape or figure. We pray you'd protect our sons from that kind of destructive thinking, and that if they're tempted to take these kinds of drastic measures, that you'd send someone in their lives to stop them. Help them to remember over and over that their identity is not in how they look on the outside but what you see as their potential and worth on the inside. We pray that our children would treasure their health as a gift from God and that they would have a passion to eat nutritious food and to stay active in order to do their part to take care of this treasure.

A prayer for your sons self-worth

Dear Jesus, help my son know that we are all born as sinners and separated from God because of our wicked hearts. However, at an early age, him grasp the life-transforming concept that he does not have to live as a sinner under that condemnation.

Teach my son that he has the opportunity to accept a new, beautiful identity that is called “good,” not because of what he has done or what he looks like, but because he is secure in who YOU say they are: treasured, delightful, known and protected. Let him not place their self-worth in accomplishments he may or may not achieve but let him discover these deeper truths about who You believe he is and build every decision he makes on that sure foundation.

A prayer for protection over your son

Lord, I pray Your emotional, physical, and spiritual protection over my son. Keep evil far from him and help him to trust You as his refuge and strength. I pray You will guard his mind from harmful instruction and grant him discernment to recognize truth. I pray You will make him strong and courageous in the presence of danger, recognizing that You have overcome and will set right all injustice and wrong one day. Help him to find rest in Your shadow, as he lives in the spiritual shelter You provide for him. Let him know that the only safe place is in Jesus, and that his home on earth is only temporary.

Prayer for your son's purity

Lord, I pray that You will create in my son a clean heart and that You would constantly renew a right spirit within him, keeping his thoughts and actions pure and motivated by love. Guard him from temptation and let him know You are always faithful to give him a way out and help to endure. May the words of his mouth and the meditations of his heart always please you and edify others.

Romans 8:28

And we know that all things work together for good to them that love God, to them who are the called according to his purpose.

www.ingramcontent.com/pod-product-compliance
Lightning Source LLC
LaVergne TN
LVHW052114160826
845678LV00015B/3548

9798375182360